FIDE SED CUI VIDE.

William Hulme's Grammar School,
MANCHESTER.
Fourth Form Chemistry
PRIZE

M. Standring

Headmaster.

Midsummer, 1975

DIESELS ON THE DEVON MAIN LINE

DIESELS

ON THE
DEVON MAIN LINE

H. L. FORD

D. BRADFORD BARTON LTD.

Frontispiece: A friendly wave for the photographer from the crew of Class 52 D 1047 *Western Lord*, heading the 08.40 Penzance to Paddington on 15 July 1972. The setting is the cutting immediately east of Teignmouth station where innumerable photographs of G W R and Western Region locomotives—steam and diesel—have been taken over the years. [Norman E. Preedy]

© *copyright D. Bradford Barton Ltd 1974*

printed in Great Britain by Chapel River Press (IPC Printers), Andover, Hants

for the publishers

D. BRADFORD BARTON LTD · Trethellan House · Truro · Cornwall · England

[Photo: G. F. Bannister]

introduction

The main GWR line through Devon, built by the South Devon Railway in the 1840's, has always been one of considerable interest as regards railway operation: west of Newton Abbot are some of the most ferocious gradients tackled by any main line in the kingdom—Dainton up to 1 in 40 in both directions; Rattery, six or seven miles long, with much of it at 1 in 70 for westbound trains; and Hemerdon. facing trains in the up direction for two miles at gradients as severe as 1 in 39.

In steam days, heavy express holiday traffic each summer required the use of a large and costly stud of banking engines at Newton and Laira, for which every ton of coal had to come the long haul from distant South Wales. It was small wonder that the GWR considered electric traction in the 1930's on the lines west of Taunton. Plans also came to nought a few years later for a new route inland from near Exminster to Newton Abbot and onward from there by a longer but much less steeply graded route to Plymouth. The first of these would have by-passed the constricted coastal line where marine erosion and landslips presented constant problems; the second would have freed the GWR from the legacy of Brunel's short, sharp inclines which had been designed for atmospheric, and not locomotive, working.

The advent of diesel traction in the 1950's was thus unusually beneficial in providing the major operating economies long overdue in Devon, as well as further west in Cornwall. With diesels, greater power became available to tackle the banks unaided—power output, moreover, that was constant and did not leave a pair of firemen soaked in sweat by the time their train, heading fourteen coaches, had reached the summit of Rattery on a hot day in July. Far fewer diesel units were needed, due to greater availability, quite apart from the disappearance of steam bankers. The speed restrictions on curves could be eased for better-running diesels, turntables abolished, and fuel lines could take the place of the costly old coaling stages. Single-manning was also still a logical hope.

As the pilot area for full dieselisation, the lines west of Newton caught the full brunt of the early troubles which characterised the change from steam. Such a radical revolution in motive power was bound to cause a major upheaval until the operation was complete. However, footplatemen, and the staff at Laira and Newton, became used to the new diesel-hydraulics, with all their undoubted advantages and all their undoubted faults, and reliability as well as railway morale began to be a factor again. The NBL 63xx units were far from the best secondary diesel on BR and at one stage, it is said, were even used in pairs to ensure that one unit at least would reach its destination. The D8xx 'Warships' settled down to really hard work in Devon once their initial troubles were sorted out, being called on to do far more than comparable classes on other Regions. The bigger 'Westerns', after two or three years of very indifferent reliability, also improved radically after their design faults had been corrected. With 2700hp available, they had the extra 500hp over the 'Warships', which made just the difference, both in loads and recovery time on the demanding section from the Teign to the Tamar. In the up direction 'Warships' could take 400 tons, but 'Westerns' a full 525 tons, both these loads being considerably more than that of an unaided 'King', it may be said. Evidence of what a good 'Western' could do came in April 1964, at the time when the policy commenced of allocating all the class at Laira. D1027 *Western Lancer,* with a test train of seven coaches (245 tons gross) covered the 225 miles to Plymouth from Paddington in less than 200 minutes running time, observing all speed restrictions and including a stop at Exeter. This was far better than the four hours of the non-stop *Cornish Riviera Express*—double-headed west of Newton—in steam days. The 'Westerns' were regarded as considerably more powerful than the 'Kings', whilst 'Warships' were compared even more favourably with the 'Castles'. The Class 42 NBL 'Warships', it may be noted, were regarded as being nowhere near as strong as the

Swindon-built Class 43s, and more prone to trouble; D852 *Tenacious* was an exception, and said to be the best of those built in Scotland. The 'Warships' were always worked hard, and even thrived on it, once the initial troubles had been cured with their riding at speed.

The main line through Devon, from the Royal Albert Bridge at Plymouth eastward to the Somerset border at Whiteball summit—some 72 route miles—falls into three different sections of quite varied character. The line from Aller Junction to the Torbay resorts is the only 'branch' remaining; this is now truncated at Paignton, where the preserve of the Torbay Steam Railway commences and continues to Kingswear.

At Plymouth, North Road station now has a completely modern look, having been rebuilt in the 1950's and with colour light signalling installed in 1960. Out past Laira, where the big diesel maintenance depot stands by the site of the former running shed, Plympton station is no more (closed in 1959) but Hemerdon bank remains unchanged. It is quietly impressive to see and hear a 'Western' taking fourteen well-filled coaches—well over 500 tons—up the long 1 in 42 of Hemerdon, breasting the summit at almost 20mph even without the benefit of a run at the bank through Plympton.

Past Hemerdon box, the constant succession of curves then commences around the contours of the southern flanks of Dartmoor at about 400 feet above sea-level, across Slade and Blachford viaducts and so to Ivybridge. Here, still climbing gently, the line crosses a massive masonry viaduct over the wooded valley of the Erme. Below the slopes of Western Beacon, the route passes Bittaford and the naval stores sidings, to Wrangaton, which is the highest point along the line. A long curve follows to the former site of Brent station, succeeded by a mile or so more of gentle climb once again to Marley Tunnel. This marks the top of Rattery bank, which drops five miles to Totnes. The gradient steepens, from 1 in 90 or so to three miles at more than 1 in 71, with curves all the way. Approximately a level mile at the foot of the bank through Totnes, over the Dart, gives way to the four mile climb to Dainton, where the last few hundred yards are at 1 in 37. Down an equally severe gradient past the woods and the quarry at Stoneycombe, it is brakes not power that need to be applied, before the speed restriction through Aller Junction, where the Torbay lines join, on the outskirts of Newton Abbot.

The line is now again almost at sea-level and its character changes, having left behind the up-hill and down-dale, slack-infested 32 miles of route so far. Newton, since the heyday of steam, has declined greatly in importance. The running shed and locomotive works were remodelled into a diesel maintenance depot in the early 1960's but this too has gone, with these activities now concentrated at Laira. Trains to or from Plymouth and Torbay are no longer divided or combined here, as in the days when Newton marked the end of the level and the start of the hill section. Lighter trains and more of them are the rule today, and the era of the sixteen-coach combined Plymouth and Paignton expresses behind 'Kings' are but a memory; the loop west of Aller Junction, formerly in constant use by the freight bankers, is now virtually redundant.

Past Hackney goods yard over the Teign, the line proceeds on the level close alongside the estuary. After Shaldon Bridge and the wharves of Teignmouth, there is a succession of bridges by Teignmouth station with its impressive stone-lined cuttings. A curve leads thence on to the sea-wall, a narrow man-made ledge between the open sea and the steeply sloping cliffs.

The mile-long promenade from here to Parson's Tunnel is a favourite walk for holidaymakers, and a well-known venue for more than one generation of railway photographers. In winter, with an onshore gale, the aspect here can be very different from the sunlit calm of summer. Parson's Tunnel is the first of five short bores—from west to east, Parson's Tunnel (374 yards), Clerk's Tunnel (60 yards), Phillott Tunnel (50 yards), Coryton (230 yards), and Kennaway Tunnel (210 yards)—through the headlands where the red Devon sandstone meets the sea along this section. With such a setting of sea, sand and strikingly coloured cliffs, topped by pines and exotic gardens, it is hardly surprising that this is perhaps the best known mile or two anywhere west of Paddington.

Dawlish station, right on the sea-front, catches the worst of southerly winter gales as well, and heavy spray often comes clear across both tracks at high tide. The ballast is enclosed by wire mesh to provide some protection against wash-outs by wave action on the seaward side. The inland 'by-pass' line proposed by the GWR in the 1930's from Exminster round to Newton was intended to avoid this exposed coastal section. After Dawlish, there follows about another mile in which the rampart of cliffs diminishes steadily in height towards Langstone Rock until they disappear altogether to merge into the flat, sandy spit of land at Dawlish Warren. At this point the line swings northwards to follow the western side of the Exe estuary. Through Dawlish Warren station, with its ageing wooden platforms and fencing, sunbleached and sagging, there are long running loops which give the impression of a four-track section.

Close beside the tide-line of the estuary, the track curves along a low sea-wall with distant views across the water towards Exmouth. At Starcross, with its small platform and shelter on the down side, there is a ferry which runs over to the latter. Continuing on the level, through Exminster—one-time site of water troughs—the lush water-meadows at the head of the Exe estuary are passed, speed here being usually well up to the 80's. On approaching Exeter, St. Thomas station is next reached. This once had a wooden over-all roof but is now a mere halt for DMUs with the remaining buildings derelict and untidy. By contrast, St. Davids is relatively unchanged in the station area, with the centre platforms used for Waterloo traffic and onward DMUs for the remaining North Devon line. The two handsome signal boxes still survive, along with a fine array of lower quadrants, while the road crossing at the up end of the platforms, leading to Riverside goods yard, is as busy as ever. Alas, the steam shed is now only a memory, the coal stage and turntable having gone and only the walls of the running shed itself remain for the diesels that are now stabled here.

At Cowley Bridge Junction, a mile or so from St. Davids, the now single line swings off across the Exe away from the main lines. On the latter, fast running from here is the order of the day, with up trains on the long but initially gentle climb through Silverton and Tiverton Junction to the last couple of miles at 1 in 115 to Whiteball Tunnel, which marks the Somerset border. For down trains, the long descent into Devon west from Whiteball is a fast twenty mile run to Cowley Bridge, which gives drivers the chance of some useful recovery time from any previous delays. Near Cullompton, part of the new motorway into the south-west runs alongside the line for something like two miles, giving motorists a fine close-up and moving panorama of WR diesel-hauled expresses at speed.

The Royal Albert Bridge at Saltash, seen here from the level of the Tamar at low tide, carries the main line over this river which forms the county boundary between Cornwall and Devon. This bridge, built by Brunel, was opened by the Prince Consort in May 1859. With two 455ft central spans high enough for naval men-o'-war to pass beneath and a total length, including the seventeen approach spans, of 730 yards, this was an immense engineering feat for its day. Each main span comprises an arch formed by a massive tube from which the bridge deck itself is slung by chains, the total weight of each being in excess of 1,000 tons. Considerable strengthening was carried out in 1905 and steel girders replaced the wrought iron ones on the approaches in 1928, but the main structure is still largely as it was in Brunel's day. In 1967 work was commenced to strengthen the bridge and extend its lease of life, partly as a precaution against the inevitable toll of age and partly to enable heavier freight trains with up to 25 ton axle-loads to be worked over it. As a vital link in the railway network west of Plymouth, the bridge—variously known as the Tamar, Saltash, Brunel and Royal Albert—will one day pose a re-building headache of major proportions to Western Region. [H. L. Ford]

One of the fleet of Newton Abbot-based 'Warships' brings an up express from Penzance off the Royal Albert Bridge into Devon in June 1969. On the right is the new suspension bridge carrying the A38 road. This was opened in 1951 alongside Brunel's original, and new high-level views of the latter are now possible from its pedestrian walkways. [H. L. Ford]

9

...800 *Sir Brian Robertson*
...as the first of the D8xx
...'arships' and broke the
...therwise orderly sequence
... naming of the class.
...tering service in July
...58 and stationed at Laira
...m September onwards,
...e is seen here at Ply-
...outh (North Road)
...th the down 'Cornish
...viera Express' early in
...59. The three-number
...de was then a recent
...roduction on Western
...gion and a forerunner
... the present four digit
...oorting codes. The first
...ure, 4, signified a
...rmouth or Penzance
...stination. The original
...rth Road station was
...ened in 1877 and a
...surely rebuilding of it was
... progress at the outbreak
... war in 1939. A much more
...bitious reconstruction
...d modernisation scheme
...as commenced in 1956
...cluding a new 10-storey
...ice block, completed
...1961. [Norman E. Preedy]

Class 52 D1066 *Western
Prefect* waits at Platform 8
at North Road for the run
westward to Truro and
Penzance on a wet and
windswept day in October
1973. Multi-aspect colour
light signalling was introduced at Plymouth in 1960,
a new box at the western
end of the station replacing
six old manual boxes. The
designation 'North Road'
was officially dropped in
1958, following the closure
of Plymouth (Friary), but
still persists.   [H. L. Ford]

Line-up at Laira in August 1959: A1A-A1A 'Warship' D601 *Ark Royal* alongside the first two of the North British D63xx class. The WR lines in Devon and Cornwall cut their teeth on these two NBL types—and a rather painful teething it was. One of the causes of the trouble is discernible in this illustration, with clearly inadequate stabling and servicing conditions for units which required very different maintenance work than 'Castles' and 'Halls'. Initially two roads of the four-road 'straight' steam shed were allocated to the new diesels, in 1958, followed by the other pair of roads eighteen months later. The new diesel maintenance depot here, able to carry out heavy servicing, was opened in the early 1960's.

[Horace H. Bleads]

Approaching Laira from the East, the lines run alongside the tidal reaches of the River Plym on the outskirts of Plymouth. A 'Western' brings a freight towards the A38 bridge in August 1973, when road widening was in progress. The two tracks on the right lead back into Laira depot and carriage sidings

[H. L. Ford]

With thirteen coaches on, B R-Sulzer Class 46 No. 139 slowly tops the severe climb of Hemerdon bank, under Sparkwell Bridge, with train 1M85, Penzance to Liverpool, in June 1973. The two miles or so at 1 in 42 from near Plympton to the summit by Hemerdon signal box, are the worst that face east-bound trains anywhere from Penzance to Paddington. The load limit, unassisted, is 515 tons for locomotives of Class 52 and 47; 465 tons for Class 45/66 and 400 tons for the 'Warships'. As an interesting comparison, in steam days a 'King' was allowed 385 tons and a 'Castle' 325 tons, figures which show the superiority of the diesel up gradients such as these. [H. L. Ford]

A down express passing the stop board at the top of Hemerdon. The run down the bank does not have the speed restrictions as on Dainton or Rattery and speeds touching ninety down to Plympton are not unknown. Acceleration down the bank, with a heavy express, can be impressive.

[H. L. Ford]

1016 *Western Gladiator* gets into her stride again on the short level stretch after the climb of Hemerdon with the 9.10 Plymouth–Paignton, August 1973. Most of the trains on this route, reversing at Newton Abbot, are worked by DMUs.

[H. L. Ford]

1069 *Western Vanguard* on a Bristol–Plymouth train passing Hemerdon box, against a distant backdrop of Dartmoor on a hazy June morning. Bankers in steam days dropped off up trains here, all freights being provided with rear-end assistance and most heavy passenger trains being piloted through to Newton Abbot. The running loops here were busy on Saturdays in summer, used by locals and freights to avoid disruption of the numerous holiday expresses.

[H. L. Ford]

Class 45 No. 70 *The Royal Marines* round the curves through the former site of Ivybridge station (closed in 1959) with a freight for Plymouth. The sheeted wagon on the left has been loaded with china clay from the nearby pits on Dartmoor; a small road-served elevator is used here for loading on this solitary remaining siding at Ivybridge. [H. L. Ford

Laira depot, which now serves all of Devon and Cornwall, has recently received a number of Class 25 BR-Sulzer units for subsidiary freight workings. One of these, No. 7573, rounds the severe curve west of Ivybridge on a working from Plymouth (Friary) to Exeter (Riverside).

[H. L. Ford]

A down parcels train from Bristol, headed by a Class 46, slows for the curve leading on to Ivybridge viaduct.   [H. L. Ford]

The wooded valley of the River Erme is spanned at Ivybridge by a masonry viaduct which is very reminiscent of those in Cornwall. Between its arches can be seen the older stone piers of the original Brunel viaduct; the rebuilding was in 1893.

[H. L. Ford]

A BR-Sulzer Class 46 running light towards Laira over the viaduct is seen from the one-time site Ivybridge up platform. Beyond is Stowford House on the slopes of the Moor, with Western Beacon on the skyline.

[H. L. For

Brush Class 47 diesel-electrics handle many of the faster air-braked Inter-City expresses to and from Cornwall; one of them heads into the morning sun with twelve coaches for Paddington in the summer of 1973, crossing Blachford Viaduct near Cornwood. The valleys draining south from Dartmoor cross the east-west route of the line and are responsible for its sinuous nature, though this is not as marked as in Cornwall. [H. L. Ford]

A down express heads west through Brent in July 1973. The section of line throug here was doubled in 1893, at the same date that the branch was opened from Bre down to Kingsbridge. This was closed in 1963. [H. L. For

Dartmoor mists shroud the remnants of Brent station as freshly-painted D1052 *Western Viceroy* passes through in June 1969 with a down train. [S. Creer]

West of Brent there is a long running loop on the up side, one of several on both lines between Exeter and Plymouth, which were installed to increase traffic capacity on busy summer Saturdays. A Class 46, running light, passes this in April 1973.   [H. L. Ford]

Marley Tunnel, near the summit of Rattery bank, has twin bores—the legacy of the long delayed provision of a second line on the South Devon Railway. The original tunnel dates from the late 1840's and its 869 yard length was necessary only on account of a local landowner whose mansion would otherwise have enjoyed a view of the line. The second bore alongside it was provided in 1891. The shallow depth of the ground above the portals at this, the eastern end, is very apparent.   [H. L. Ford]

NBL Class 22 D 6314 piloting D 801 *Vanguard* with the up 'Cornish Riviera Express' near Tigley signal box on Rattery, August 1961. Approaching with a freight for Plymouth is another 'Warship', D 829 *Magpie*. This was the era before yellow warning panels were painted on the ends of diesels, from 1962 onwards.   [R. E. Toop]

n the 1 in 90 descent of Rattery bank down to Totnes; D 1035 *Western Yeoman* (above) cautiously
ropping down the gradient on the up line with 'The Cornishman' on a Sunday in June 1969, due to p.w.
ork; and Class 45 D 18 (below) coasting down with 13 coaches bound for Manchester in July 1973.
ne cleaner ballast on the down-hill line contrasts with that on the left where locomotives are moving
ore slowly and at full power.   [H. L. Ford]   25

A pair of 'Warships'
at the same point in
August 1962, making
light work of the
climb with 4,400hp
available and a mere
nine-coach load.
[R. E. Toop]

26

...e of the Laira 'Westerns' runs down the curving 1 in 47 stretch towards Totnes on
...e lower part of Rattery bank. The track here, as at Hemerdon, was laid double from
...e outset, to avoid the long delays there would otherwise have been to all traffic.

[H. L. Ford]

The severe curve under the road bridge into Totnes station right at the foot of Rattery calls for caution, particularly
for trains that stop here and have to turn into the platform road. Here the brakes come off and power is put back on
as one of the named Class 46s heads 'The Cornishman' north-bound for Leeds in 1971.   [Malcolm Dunnett]

The down 'Cornishman' sweeps past Totnes station on the through road, ready for the long climb ahead but still far from flat out because of the speed restrictions. With thirteen on, speed will drop back to something like 20mph by the time No. 125 is three miles further on, passing Tigley box. On the left is the creamery which still provides considerable milk tank traffic from Totnes, whilst under the footbridge can be seen the distinctive signal box with its bay-window.

[H. L. Ford]

After a stop at Totnes to shunt some wagons into the down siding, D1025 *Western Guardsman* eases onto the main line to begin the climb of Rattery with a long freight for St. Blazey. She is not yet on full power as the clear exhausts from her two Maybach engines show; another few hundred yards, however, and their distinctive growl will begin to sound fairly widely across the Devon countryside as she works up to maximum tractive effort.

[H. L. Ford]

The familiar outline of a 'Western' on a down freight crossing the aged bridge over a tributary of the River Dart at Littlehempston, east of Totnes.

[H. L. Ford]

An air-braked Class 47
with the down 'Cornish
Riviera Express'
heads towards Totnes
on a July afternoon
in 1973. Alas head-
boards have dis-
appeared—quite
unaccountably—from
the present day railway
scene. The 'Limited',
as this express has
always been known to
railwaymen since its
inception in 1904, still
has a limited load, as
in steam days.

[H. L. Ford]

Class 33 BRCW diesel-electrics in the 65xx series, from Southern Region, now occasionally work to Plymouth and are regularly seen at Exeter. Here No. 6500, first of the class, from Eastleigh depot, heads a train of empty oil tanks halfway up the climb to Dainton, en route to Fawley. The sharp curves along this section of line are self-evident in this view near the A381 road bridge. [H. L. Ford]

Dainton bank, and the tunnel at its summit, is perhaps the best known locality on the entire Devon main line. It is quite a short, but very steep climb in each direction, something like 2½ miles either way to the summit, from sea level to about 300ft. In either direction the approach to the tunnel is at 1 in 36 or 1 in 37, making Dainton a serious operational problem in the steam era. An up freight, headed by a 'Western', nears the summit in August 1973.

[H. L. Ford]

No outward sign of the adverse gradient is apparent from this 'Western' on an up express at Dainton, compared to the sound and the fury that would have been evident from a 'Hall' or 'Castle'. No longer do firemen toil heroically to keep up steam on these South Devon banks and no longer do Newton Abbot or Laira have to maintain a costly stud of bankers. Few, if any, passenger turns are now double-headed, although the use of 'Warships' in pairs was seen for a time in the late 1960's. 'Westerns' and Class 47s are permitted to take 525 tons west from Newton Abbot without assistance, Class 45/46 up to 490 tons, and Class 42 'Warships' 415 tons. [H. L. Ford]

D1007 *Western Talisman* growls past Dainton Sidings box in August 1973 with freight 7C52 from S Blazey to Severn Tunnel Junction. The sidings on the down side have now gone, the former GW sign box has been replaced by a modern box-like structure, and only a short length of the up siding remain The superb lush setting of the Devon countryside alone remains unchanged. [H. L. For

A decade and more ago, D603 *Conquest* west of the tunnel on a Paddington–Penzance train in March 1961. [W. L. Underhay] Below, Class 45 No. 30, running light towards Newton Abbot. [H. L. Ford]

Framed in the portal of Dainton Tunnel, D1065 *Western Consort*, heading west. As she tops the summit, full power is shut off and one can hear plainly the distinctive soft whistling sound of the two engines as the revs die away to idling.

[H. L. Ford]

CATCH POINTS
698 YARDS

A Penzance–Paddington express gathers speed on the steep gradient away from the cutting on the tunnel's eastern side. The line can be seen curving away towards Stoneycombe, and Aller Junction beyond.

[H. L. Ford]

A very different engine beat comes from the heavy Class 45s low-speed Sulzer unit as she tops the rise; No. 22, from Holbeck shed, on the 9.15 Liverpool (Lime Street) to Penzance, September 1973. The unusually large dimensions of the tunnel portal are noteworthy; a few yards inside it tapers downwards to more normal proportions. Its length is relatively short and the signalman in the box has a clear view through it.

[H. L. Ford]

D1066 *Western Prefect* and D1041 *Western Prince* doubleheading a heavy train of loaded tank wagons past Dainton box. A few exceptional freights still receive the assistance of a second locomotive on the Newton Abbot–Plymouth section but incomparably fewer than in the era of steam. The reporting code of the pilot locomotive has remained unchanged since a previous working. [H. L. Ford]

A Paddington–Penzance train passing Stoneycombe quarries in July 1973. In the sidings, loaded hoppers await collection, considerable traffic in ballast emanating here for Western Region. The signal box (left) has a reinforced roof and windows protected by wire mesh as a precaution against flying stones during blasting in the quarries, which lie close on either side of the tracks.   [H. L. Ford]

Gateshead-allocated Class 46 D173 tackles the bank towards Stoneycombe with a Manchester to Plymouth train in September 1970 on a well kept section of newly ballasted bullhead track. The 50mph restriction sign is typical of the innumerable service slacks that exist west of Aller Junction. [H. L. Ford]

A distant view of a down freight headed by a 'Western' amid the woods and fields around Stoneycombe. [H. L. Ford]

D830 *Majestic*, with a rake of rather assorted coaching stock, near the foot of Dainton with a Swansea Penzance train on 30 March 1961. The class looked its best in this original green rather than in the alternative livery of maroon or rail blue. [W. L. Underhay]

First of the class, D1000 *Western Enterprise* approaching Aller Junction with the 8.30 a.m. Plymouth Paddington in February 1962. She had then been in service at Laira only a month and was resplendent in experimental 'golden sand' livery with red buffer beams. [W. L. Underhay]

D829 *Magpie* between Aller and Stoney-combe with a Liverpool–Plymouth express in 1962.
[W. L. Underhay]

D1049 *Western Monarch* on the curve at Aller Junction with empty ballast hoppers consigned to Stoney-combe quarry sidings. The track on the right was the loop used by trains awaiting steam bankers westward toward Plymouth.

[H. L. Ford]

Class 47 No. 1760 on a down express for Plymouth passes the lower quadrants west of Aller Junction. Colour light signals are, alas, now in process of installation along much of the Devon main line.

[H. L. Ford]

A 'Warship' and a 'Peak' running in harness past Aller Junction with the r... bound 'Devonian' 1971. This junctio... of the lines to Tor... and Plymouth is a ... known locality am... railway photo- graphers.

[Malcolm Dun...

In the period of transition from steam to diesel, double- heading by the two forms of tractive power was not uncommon but banking of freights by diesels was rarely photographed. Here Class 22 D6325, not long out of works, helps No. 4914 *Cranmore Hall* on the way towards Dainton in October 1960.

[W. L. Underhay]

Aller Junction; a pair of D63xx class diesels on a Plymouth–Newton Abbot train in April 1961. Below: an unusual combination on the 07.31 Nottingham–Plymouth train, 5 August 1961—D6321 and 47xx Class 2-8-0 No. 4705.

[W. L. Underhay]

D806 *Cambrian* at the head of a Plymouth–Exeter train in July 1961. [W. L. Underhay] Below: D1051 *Western Ambassador* coming off the Torquay line with 2B81, from Paignton to Exeter, September 1973. [H. L. Ford]

The Class 52 'Westerns' had their early troubles in service, particularly with torque convertors and bogies, but then settled down to give good service. Their loss from the Devon railway scene will be mourned far and wide. Here D1064 *Western Regent* sweeps under the signal gantry, cleared for the Plymouth line, with an express for Cornwall at Whitsun 1973.   [H. L. Ford]

rush Class 47 No. 1697, in two-tone green livery, heads past Aller Junction with a
eturning day excursion from Paignton to Birmingham.   [G. F. Gillham]

600 *Active* on the down 'Torbay Express' passing Aller Junction in September 1959,
te and still losing time. The first A1A-A1A 'Warships' had a hard time of it when pitched
to the deep end with the Laira enginemen who loved their dependable 'Castles'
nd 'Halls'.   [Derek Cross]

On the Torbay line, D824 *Highflyer* climbs the 1 in 55 bank from Torre to Torquay with the 8.00 a.m. Kingswear–Paddington train, August 1960.

[W. L. Underhay]

The last mile or so of the Kingswear branch is alongside the River Dart, providing a superb setting now enjoyed by steam enthusiasts on the Torbay Steam Railway. In April 1961, years before Western Region considered terminating their trains at Paignton, D813 *Diadem* approaches Britannia Halt with the down 'Torbay Express'.

[W. L. Underhay]

807 *Caradoc* leaving Torre with a Paddington–Kingswear train in August 1962.

[W. L. Underhay]

Scenes at Kingswear, terminus of the fourteen mile 'branch' from Aller Junction, serving the resorts of Torbay; Class 35 'Hymek' D7049 arriving with a short freight in September 1963.

[R. E. Toop]

Another 'Hymek', D7071, with a train for Newton Abbot, near Churston on 5 August 1964.

[R. E. Toop]

D6333 arriving at Kingswear with empty coaching stock. The quay and railway facilities here were radically extended in 1904. Dartmouth, across the river, enjoyed Great Western service via the ferry.

[R. E. Toop]

826 *Jupiter* ready to leave ngswear for Paddington April 1961. [H. H. Bleads]

'Western' alongside the dal estuary of the Dart ith a down train.
[South Devon Railway Museum]

The Beyer Peacock Class 35 diesel-hydraulics made occasional appearances in the south-west in the mid-1960's, and at one time it was proposed to have an allocation in the area. However they appeared principally on excursions and summer expresses to Torbay, from their home area of Bristol and South Wales. D7089, on 4 August 1964, heads a train from Newton Abbot towards Kingswear. As with the rest of the WR diesel-hydraulics, these 'Hymeks' have been declared non-standard and due to be phased out.

[R. E. Toop]

A rail-level view of D806 *Cambrian* in June 1961 heading the down 'Torbay Express' through the cutting near Noss Shipyard on the banks of the Dart. Inaugurated in 1923, this has always been tne principal express to the Devon resorts, dating back originally to the 1890's.

[W. L. Underhay]

D807 *Caradoc* passing the bulky castle-like outline of Torquay gas works with a morning up train from Kingswear in 1960. Weighing only 79 tons, yet with 2,200hp engines, the 'Warships' were small but big-hearted. Their naming sequence, from D804 onwards, followed an alphabetical and numerical pattern up to D870 *Zulu*.

[W. L. Underhay]

One of the D63xx class near Torre with a Paignton-bound train i 1962. The flat-nosed pug-like appearance of these diesels contraste strongly with the bulbous curved front of the 'Warships' and th heavily styled cab ends of the 'Hymeks'. [W. L. Underha

A pair of 'Hymeks', from Bristol (Bath Road) shed, D7017 and D7019, with a train of empty stock returning from Torquay to the carriage sidings at Newton Abbot. July 1962.

[W. L. Underhay]

BR-Sulzer Class 45 D71 *The Staffordshire Regiment (Prince of Wales's Own)* gets the 'board' at Paignton, to leave with the 14.35 to York. Although the date is May 1973, she still retains the D for diesel prefix which BR discontinued from January 1969 onwards. Her re-numbering will be overtaken by the new 1973 system of numbering, which incorporates the class, as in continental practice. [P. J. Lynch]

A return to the main line at Newton Abbot for a striking night study of D838 *Rapid* at the head of the 2.30 a.m. Paddington to Penzance, 21 December 1962. D838 was one of the NBL-built 'Warships' of Class 43 with NBL/MAN engines and Voith transmissions in place of the Bristol Siddeley-Maybach engines and Mekydro transmissions of the Swindon-built Class 42s.

[W. L. Underhay]

D806 *Cambrian* at the west end of the station with the down 'Torbay Express' in September 1959.   [Derek Cross]

D1022 *Western Sentinel* at Platform 1, beneath the distinctive signal gantry, with the 08.00 Bristol to Penzance—the correct code for which should read 1B81. The station layout here is unusual, being basically composed of two long island platforms with half the length of each face considered and numbered as a separate platform. This was to facilitate the division of trains which had portions for the Torquay and Plymouth lines, scissors crossovers being provided for this.   [H. L. Ford]

am and diesel
Newton Abbot, in
y 1962.
          [J. R. Besley]

After an adverse signal check, D1048 *Western Lady* starts a Severn Tunnel Junction freight on the move again from the up through line at Newton Abbot, alongside the Motorailer terminus. The cooling tower and chimneys of the power station here are a local landmark visible for miles.　　　　　　[H. L. Ford]

028 *Western Hussar*, from Laira, and Class 47 No. 1938, from Bristol (Bath Road), tering the station with a Penzance–Liverpool train, July 1973. Newton Abbot West x is typical of those in the area, but is due to disappear shortly, along with the fine wer-quadrant gantry.　　　　　　　　　　　　[H. L. Ford]

On the level stretch alongside the estuary of the Teign; D 823 *Hermes* (above) with a 14-coach down express in August 1960, and D 805 *Benbow* (below) with a Wolverhampton–Penzance train, March 1961.   [W. L. Underhay]

Piloting duties from Exeter or Newton Abbot through to Plymouth were regarded as useful for crew training; D6330 leads Castle Class No. 5060 *Earl of Berkeley*, on a Wolverhampton to Paignton train along the banks of the Teign on a June day in 1962.
[W. L. Underhay]

High tide in the Teign estuary on a winter's day in 1963 with a 'Warship' on an up freight. [J. R. Besley]

nother view from Shaldon
idge at low tide, with a
ass 46 on a down
press in May 1972.
[H. L. Ford]

The driver of Class 45 D 15
looks back for the 'right-
away' with the up
'Devonian' at Teignmouth,
August 1973. Holbeck-based
'Peaks' are common on this
train, as with the
'Cornishman'. [H. L. Ford]

eignmouth station is as
eat now, and as well kept,
it was in Great Western
ays, and remains very little
anged since it was built
its present form in the
80's. This is in stark
ntrast to so many other
est Country stations which
ve so obviously fallen on
rd times. An inordinate
mber of bridges cross
e railway along this short
ction of line through
eignmouth. [H. L. Ford]

Two views of D1048 *Western Lady*, with a freight again, on a winter afternoon in 1972, on the curve that brings the tracks on to the open coast. The track along the protective sea wall is a favourite with holiday-makers and a well-known vantage point for railway photographers. [H. L. Ford]

Beneath the flower-studded slope of the cliffs at Teignmouth, Class 47 No. 1713 and Class 42 D867 *Zenith* head a Saturdays-only Paignton–Manchester train in July 1969.

[Norman E. Preedy]

The up 'Mayflower', from Plymouth, sweeps under the last of the overbridges at Teignmouth in August 1959, behind D801 *Vanguard*. This express name was first introduced in June 1957, but was discontinued in 1965, along with various other WR train names, and was revived again in 1970 for a time to commemorate the 350th anniversary of the sailing of the Pilgrim Fathers from Plymouth.

[H. H. Bleads]

One of the NBL A1A-A1A 'Warships' on an up express passing Parson's Tunnel signal box (now dismantled) nestling under the cliffs east of Teignmouth, in 1960. This section of track was doubled in 1884.

[S. Creer]

High tide and a moderately rough sea along Teignmouth sea wall, from Sprey Point. This exposed section of line has always been plagued by minor cliff falls but damage to the very substantial sea wall is rare. As at Dawlish, onshore gales from a southerly quarter, and the exceptionally high tides they cause, give trouble here with heavy spray sweeping across the tracks. 'Halls' and 'Castles' could withstand this but an intake of salt-water, intermingled with sand, is not recommended for diesels.

[Malcolm Dunnett]

Class 47 No. 1657
leads a Paddington to
Newquay train out of
Parson's Tunnel, 18
August 1973. This was
opened out from its
original single line
broad gauge
dimensions to double
the standard gauge in
the early 1900's.
[Norman E. Preedy]

Five short tunnels carry the line through the red sandstone headlands and cliffs just
west of Dawlish, in a setting unrivalled in character anywhere else on the Great
Western. D1016 *Western Gladiator* leaves the easternmost of these tunnels with an
up afternoon milk train from Cornwall in July 1973.   [Norman E. Preedy]

A distant view of Dawlish and the station, in the evening at low tide. The line is right
alongside high water mark and on occasion during south-easterly gales in winter
the inner (up) line is used for all traffic because of waves breaking on the sea wall.
[H. L. Ford]

323 *Hermes* heads along the seafront at Dawlish with an freight from Ponsandane yard at Penzance. Note how the ballast on the seaward side of the down line is enclosed within wire mesh to prevent wave action causing erosion damage to the road bed.
[Norman E. Preedy]

East of Dawlish, the cliffs diminish in height to the flat sandy area around Dawlish Warren. Near Langstone Rock, dapper D843 *Sharpshooter* heads westward on a sunny Saturday in May 1971, with a train from Taunton p.w. yard, bound for Hackney and some Sunday work west of Newton Abbot.
[Norman E. Preedy]

Flanking the grounds of Powderham Castle, the line leaves the side of the estuary and heads almost in a straight line for Exeter across the level marshes and pastureland near Exminster. D832 *Onslaught*, with an up train from Kingswear in 1962, has most of the speed restrictions behind her and can now begin to show her paces.

[W. L. Underhay]

e long platforms at Dawlish Warren are a legacy of the days when this was a popular day resort with cals as well as holiday makers from farther afield. The sun-bleached wooden platforms—little changed appearance in the past fifty years—are deserted in winter. Long running loops give the impression quadruple track. [H. L. Ford]

ar Starcross, the line runs immediately alongside the Exe and at one point crosses a small tidal inlet the main estuary by an embankment and girder bridge. D1034 *Western Dragoon* heads west over this 19 September 1973, disturbing the waders feeding on the mudflats adjoining the line. [H. L. Ford]

The up end of the four track section through Exminster. Class 46 No. 141 is on the eight mark as she makes up time with a Liverpool to Penzance train—a far cry from the atmospheric system which this South Devon line first saw in the 1840's.

[G. F. Gillham]

The crew of a 'Warship' ease their charge slowly over a flooded section of track near Exminster signalbox after the Exe had overflowed its banks in September 1960. This is a hazard the line has always been subject to down the lower-lying parts of the Exe valley. This was the one-time site of the water-troughs installed in 1904 to enable the newly-introduced 'Cornish Riviera Express' and other trains to run through non-stop to Plymouth.

[W. L. Underhay]

The down 'Cornish Riviera Express' with its limited winter formation of seven coaches leaving Exeter (St. Davids) behind D847 *Strongbow* in October 1961. The headboard carries the Cornish 'One and All' coat of arms.

[W. L. Underhay]

BARROW
CROSSING
INDICATOR

Exeter (St. Davids) is the
principal railway route
centre in the West Countr
where the GWR and SR
lines crossed. The tracks
to and from Exeter (Centra
are visible top left in thes
two views at the west end
of St. Davids.   [H. L. For

NBL Class 22 'Baby Warship' D6334, in blue livery, with a down train of empty milk tanks, 8 August 1971. [Norman E. Preedy]

St. Davids as we know it today dates from a major rebuild just prior to the First World War. Its two centre platforms are used for Southern trains to and from Waterloo, and for the d.m.u.s working onwards to North Devon. In this illustration the down goods line is seen in the centre. [H. L. Ford]

1056 *Western Sultan*, in tip-top condition, waits to leave Exeter in May 1971 with a ‘addington–Paignton train. She is one of the Class 52s fitted with a small rectangular ‘entilator beneath the windscreen as an experiment to give increased ventilation in ‘e driving cab. [Norman E. Preedy]

In mint condition after a protracted overhaul at Swindon—the last main-line diesel to be overhauled there—D1023 *Western Fusilier* awaits the right-away for Reading and Paddington in September 1973. At this end of St. Davids station, there is a busy level crossing used by pedestrians and by road traffic to and from Riverside goods yard.

[H. L. Ford]

NBL Class 22 D6336 by the old water tower at the west end of the station on 8 M... 1971, heading for Riverside yard with a loose-coupled freight. She was one of the la... survivors in the class, withdrawn in January 1972 and cut up at Swindon a few mont... later.

[Norman E. Pree...

he site of the once-busy Exeter shed is now a stabling point for diesels and a signing-on or off place for
rews. Only part of the walls of the shed itself remain, together with the massive water tower at the west
nd (see page 89). Signs of the change in motive power are evident in these two views; above, in May
971, 'Warships' and Class 22 units are to be seen, some stored out of use; in June 1973, below, there
re as many diesel-electrics as diesel-hydraulics in the Type 4 line-up. [Norman E. Preedy: H. L. Ford]

The sight of a Class 45 would have been rare at St. Davids only a few years ago but now it is commonplace. No. 101,
from Holbeck, waits to depart with the up 'Cornishman', for Leeds. Up to 1970, locomotives were changed at
Bristol on almost all these north-east to south-west workings. [H. L. Ford]

039 *Western King*
ches up out of
Davids with a
ddington–
zance train in
rch 1963.
[W. L. Underhay]

Class 47 No. 1673
Cyclops brings a work
train, including
two PWM shunters,
past Cowley Bridge
Junction heading for
Exeter (Riverside).
The Southern line to
north Devon and Corn-
wall is on the left;
for some years this
was included in WR
territory. [H. L. Ford]

13 *Diadem* enter-
the station with
up 'Devonian',
ptember 1960.
is train was
ugurated in 1927.
ning to Bradford
rster Square) and
name still survives
the current time-
le—though not
the train itself. now
ning to Leeds.
[W. L. Underhay]

In April 1969 D1002 *Western Explorer* heads towards Exeter, occupying the wrong line due to engineering work, with a Liverpool–Plymouth train. The SR line (left) was singled in the 1960's and the Exe bridges re-built.

[W. L. Underhay]

Another view at Cowley Bridge Junction, across the fast-running waters of the Exe in winter, with an up express on the main line en route to Bristol.

[W. L. Underhay]

Paddington-bound D1030 *Western Musketeer* passes Class 46 No. 139, waiting to follow with a freight, on the Exeter side of Cowley Bridge Junction, October 1973.   [H. L. Ford]

On the level near Rewe, midway between Cowley Bridge and Cullompton, Class 46 D164 is near the 90mph limit with a westbound express; March 1972.
    [H. L. Ford]

Class 25 No. 7676 near Rewe with milk tanks for the Hemyock branch which leaves the main line at Tiverton Junction. [H. L. Ford]   Below: On the border of Devon and Somerset at Whiteball summit, D1061 *Western Envoy* leaves the tunnel (1,092 yards) with a Paignton train in October 1972.   [T. W. Nicholls]